TOBIAS

Philip Birmingham

TOBIAS

Philip Birmingham

Philip Birmingham

This book is a work of fiction. Places, events, and situations in this story are purely fictional. Any resemblance to actual persons, living or dead, is coincidental.

© Copyright March 2008 by Philip Birmingham. All rights reserved.

No part of this book may be reproduced, stored in a retrieval system, or transmitted by any means, electronic, mechanical, photocopying, recording, or otherwise, without written permission from the author.

ISBN 978-0-557-05293-6

Chapter One

Tobias worked for the most unique healer since Christ, and one whose very existence was known by relatively few people. He leaned back in his office chair amid his new surroundings and ran his hands over the old oak desk that came with the building. It had a musty smell to it, the same as the entire room. Years upon years of dust permeated every pore of the walls and floor. The room was on the second floor of a two-story brick structure built at the turn of the century. It had seen an endless array of tenants over the years; lawyers, accountants, an investment firm, beauty parlor, several importers, and on and on. It had been vacant and up for sale for almost two years, and was offered free of charge for the healer's use until it was sold. Usually Tobias would choose a first floor location to accommodate the infirm, but this particular building was the only one that was available.

Tobias swiveled his chair to the left in response to the sound of several pigeons landing on the outside window sill. They immediately began cooing animatedly and scrabbling for position. He observed there were four, and after listening carefully for several minutes he could identify each one by its distinctive sound. He leaned forward and touched the grime-crusted window with his finger. The pigeons twittered and shuffled, but none of them flew away.

The sound of the door opening on the first floor caused him to swivel back to face the head of the stairs. The game began. He listened for the footsteps as his instinctive second nature took over and ran aural calculations in his mind. He knew there were twelve steps, and based on the sounds he guessed it was a man, weight about one hundred fifty pounds. The footsteps were pronounced and energetic. *Good,* thought Tobias, *it's probably not serious.*

The man reached the top and stopped. He looked at the empty wooden chair that had been placed in the alcove at the head of the stairs, then glanced across the room to where Tobias sat, noting that there was no chair beside the desk. Tobias knew exactly what the man was thinking.

"Please, take a seat," Tobias said. "I know it's a little unusual, but I prefer interviewing people from a distance. I hope you don't mind." The man shrugged, cleared his throat, and sat down.

"No, I guess not," the man continued, assuming that the chair was placed there to provide a safe distance from anyone with a contagious disease. "Are you the healer?"

"No, my name is Tobias. I work for the healer. He's in the room behind me." Tobias judged the man's age to be mid-thirties. "May I inquire as to the nature of your problem?"

"Yes, of course, of course." The man seemed hesitant to reply, which Tobias picked up on immediately.

"If it's something of a personal nature, something that might be uncomfortable to discuss, I can assure you that nothing about your problem will ever leave this room."

"No," the man replied, "I'm just a little embarrassed to discuss it." The man cleared his throat again. "I feel a little ill at ease. I don't have a great problem, but I can't seem to find a doctor, or a medicine, that will cure me."

"How did you find the healer?" Tobias queried. "We've only been here two days."

"I don't remember exactly," the man quickly answered, looking puzzled. "I was discussing my problem with a coworker, and he said he knew someone, and then that guy knew someone else…that kind of thing. Why do you ask?" Tobias adjusted his tinted eyeglasses, pushing them farther up on his nose.

"Just curious. We find a location and tell no one, and within a couple of days the word gets out somehow, and then people begin showing up. Soon, by word of mouth, the crowds get bigger and bigger, and in no time at all they get unmanageable. Fighting invariably breaks out at some point, and then it becomes necessary to move again. Since we don't tell anyone where we move, I always marvel at how quickly they find us." Tobias sensed the man was getting agitated.

"Why do you move?" the man asked. "Are you trying to hide from people?"

"No." Tobias answered, "Quite the contrary. It's just that by using this method the healer can cure more people in a given period of time before the crowds get ugly. If we announce where we're moving to, the crowds follow us right away. We've been doing it this way for years."

"Fine, I guess," the man commented. "So, what's the deal here?"

"Deal?" said Tobias. "What are you talking about?"

"How does it work? What's the charge? Why are you here? What's your job?"

"I screen all those who come here for healing."

"So you decide who gets in and who gets the boot?"

"Only to the extent that I screen out the incurables. Other than that, my instructions from the healer are to refuse no one. As for the charge, there is none, but you can leave a donation if you're so inclined." The man leaned forward in the chair.

"Incurables? Like what?"

"Retardation, for one," Tobias replied. "The healer can do nothing for them, and allowing them to see the healer is just giving their caregivers false hope. I explain that to them and send them away. May I ask how old you are?"

"Do you need that before I can be cured?" the man asked, furrowing his brow. "I don't mean to be rude, but I just wonder why that's needed, and why all the questions." Tobias felt the heavy skepticism.

"No, I don't need that before you can see the healer. I don't need anything, actually, other than the nature of your problem. I was just curious."

The man fidgeted in the chair, then cleared his throat again. "I…it's a rash. I know, I know, that's hardly a reason to seek a healer, but I can't get rid of it. It covers most of my body, but thankfully not my face or hands. I've had it for years. I lose a lot of sleep, and I can't relax for more than a few minutes before it flares up. It itches and pains me at the same time. I've tried everything…everything. Home remedies, advice from every friend and family member, all kinds of folk remedies and old wives tales, and a host of doctors. I've spent a fortune on prescriptions and…"

"That's enough," Tobias interrupted. "I just needed some general information from you." Tobias was relieved that the problem was minor. It would take little or no virtue from the healer to cure.

"Don't you need to know what the doctors diagnosed?" the man asked.

"No, it doesn't make any difference."

"I'm thirty-four...My name is Anthony...Tony."

Tobias smiled. "The healer is in the room behind me, but I need to tell you some things, so you won't be shocked."

"Oh...shocked? Is it about the cost, or should I say the donation?" Tobias concealed his own irritation.

"No. I told you, there is no cost, none whatsoever. I need to tell you what to expect when you open that door."

"Yeah?" the man responded nervously.

"Every cure the healer effects takes virtue from him."

"Virtue? Whaddya mean virtue?"

"Health, for want of a better term. Each cure reduces his health. The more serious the illness, the more it takes from him."

"My God...I'm sorry to hear that. I wouldn't have come to him if it was something that would hurt him."

"Don't be concerned about it," Tobias replied. "In fact the healer has instructed me not to tell anyone that, but I made an exception in your case because if you're cured, it shouldn't have any adverse effect at all."

"Well, that's good to hear," the man replied. "Is there anything else?" Tobias debated about not telling him more, but decided he didn't like the man, and wanted him gone as soon as possible. A guilt trip was in order.

"All of the healings he has done, especially the serious ones, have taken a toll. He's done this for years, and now his body is contorted and his weight is dangerously low. For every spinal deformity he's cured, he suffers a degree of spinal deformity himself. For every lung disease he's cured, he loses some lung capacity. You get the idea, I'm sure. He's emaciated, and he can barely speak above a whisper. In short, you'll find his appearance shocking." There was a pause of several seconds before the man spoke.

"What do I do?" Tobias then gave the man the canned speech he had used so often.

"You simply walk in the room. The healer is on a cot, and there is a chair beside it. Go and sit in that chair. You don't need to speak, or even introduce yourself. Just sit and wait. The healer will open his eyes and smile at you. Wait for him to extend his hand. When he does, take it, and simply hold his hand loosely in your own. He needs to touch you. When he closes his eyes, you close yours. If there is to be a cure it will come within minutes. You may have some pain, which will depend on how serious your condition is, and what healing is taking place within your body. Do not jerk your hand away, or cry out in any way. If you do not sense anything at all within one minute, release his hand. That will mean that no cure has taken place. In some rare cases, however, the healing does take place at a later time, but generally it does not. Do you understand what I've told you so far?"

"Yes...yeah, I suppose. I really feel bad about this now."

But I'm guessing you'll go ahead with it anyway, Tobias thought.

"Is there anything else?" the man asked. "Do you need my full name, or any other information?"

"No, take all the time you need, and go in when you're ready." A few seconds of silence followed, more fidgeting, and then the man rose and walked across the floor. As he approached, a scent registered in Tobias' nostrils. *Expensive cologne,* he noted. *A professional man, makes good money... wearing a dress suit.* The man cleared his throat again as he passed Tobias. *Five foot six, maybe five foot seven,* Tobias guessed. He heard the knob turn behind him as the man entered the room and closed the door behind him.

The sound of the pigeons cooing caused Tobias to turn back to the window. They were still on the sill outside. He listened for a few minutes, then cocked his head to one side as he concentrated, confirming his previous observation. Four different voices. Two sounded almost the same, but one of them had a slightly different cadence. The voices of the other two were distinctly different. Tobias sat back in the old chair with a satisfied grin. He loved the soft, gurgling sounds they made.

He had held pigeons before and liked their feel and shape. He loved to pet them. His thoughts went back to when he was a child and his grandmother gave him a paper bag of moistened stale bread to feed them. She felt bad giving them dry bread without some water.

He would sit on a bench in the little park across from his house while they landed on his lap and shoulders, and anywhere else they could find room on the bench. He remembered feeling he was doing good things for God's creatures when they ate greedily from his hand. Some cooing and animated movement brought him back to the present, and told him the pigeons on the sill were now bickering over something. Even their fights were gentle.

He was getting hunger pangs in his stomach, telling him that the time was close to twelve. *Where's Stephanie?* He wondered. *She's usually here by eleven-thirty.*

Another five minutes passed, and then the door behind him opened and the man emerged. Tobias said nothing until the man walked across the floor and reached the head of the stairs.

"How'd it go, Anthony?"

"Yes, yes…it was fine…it went well." The man's voice was different. He spoke more slowly than before. The nervousness was gone, and the tone was more relaxed, more respectful, and obviously awe-filled. A cure had been affected. He wondered if the man would even say thank you. He decided to remain silent and say nothing.

"Thank you."

"For what?" Tobias replied quickly.

"I'm cured. I felt it happen. It's gone…all those years of suffering and embarrassment. Gone…gone in a few seconds. Somehow I know it's gone for good. Thank you."

"Why are you thanking me? I didn't do anything."

"I…I don't know. I was very moved by his physical condition. He took my hand, just as you said, and smiled at me. Then he closed his eyes, and right away I felt the change taking place inside and outside my body. I could feel it! I could actually feel it! A few seconds later it stopped, and then he dropped my hand. His eyes were closed, and I didn't want to disturb him any more, so I just sat there for awhile. My God, it's gone…it's gone. This is beyond incredible. I'm very skeptical about this kind of stuff, but my God…Thank God."

"God?" Tobias commented. "The hard evidence is the healer and you, who are now cured. Did you see God? Did He speak to you, Anthony, when you were in the room?"

"I don't understand. What are you saying, that I was cured by some other power or force?"

"What I'm saying is that neither you nor I know what cured you. The healer would tell you it was God working through him, but in fact even he doesn't know. Maybe he just has powers that are different from other humans, or maybe anyone can cure themselves if they have enough faith."

"I can't believe what I'm hearing, Mr…Mr…"

"Tobias, my name is Tobias."

"It has to be God that cured me."

"No it doesn't. It could have been yourself." Tobias decided he had made the man uncomfortable enough. "Go in peace, Anthony, and I'm truly glad you were cured. And please don't tell anyone where we're located. Would you promise me that?"

"Yes...yes, thank you." The man started to descend the stairs. After a few steps down he stopped and paused momentarily, then resumed walking to the bottom and out the door.

We don't need the money, but it would have been nice if the bastard offered to donate something, Tobias mused. *Where the hell is Stephanie?*

As if on cue he heard the downstairs door open and close again, then footsteps on the stairs. He knew it was she. He faced Stephanie when she appeared at the head of the stairs.

"Hi, Toby!" came her cheerful voice. "I've got some lunch for you!" She was a plump, middle-aged woman in her mid-forties who wore a hairdo from the fifties. She had a round, ruddy face with an infectious smile, and a disposition to match. She was one of the few people permitted to call him Toby.

"Hi Steph, what time is it?" She walked across the floor toward the desk. "I meant to mention it before, but you've lost some weight," he added. There was the rustle of paper bags and the click of paper cups being placed on the desk.

"It's almost twelve, Toby. How do you do it? Yes, yes, I have lost some weight. How much would you say?"

"What does your scale say? I'd be guessing."

"I think I would rather believe you than my scale. So, go ahead, tell me how much."

"Okay," Tobias answered, taking up the challenge. "Walk back and forth for a bit." Her response was immediate, and he cocked his head to one side as she strode back and forth from the desk to the top of the stairs. "Slower," he urged. She slowed her pace and made the walk again, finally stopping in front of his desk.

"Well?" she said, grinning at him.

"Did you see the guy that just left?" Tobias asked.

"Yes, and I saw the look on his face. He was cured of something, wasn't he?"

"Yeah, and he and I had a little theological discussion. I guess I shocked him a little."

"Oh, Toby, you didn't. Why do you do that? Just because you're an atheist doesn't mean you have any right to attack anyone else's faith."

"For the umpteenth time, I'm not an atheist. I'm probably more of an agnostic…maybe a pagan."

"Well, keep it to yourself, Toby. You really shouldn't shake anyone's faith, especially after they're dramatically cured by the healer."

Tobias drummed his fingers softly on the desk. "I guess you're right, Steph. Some people need that simple faith and belief in a deity. I don't, but I shouldn't challenge anyone else's faith in an absolute God. Then again, you know I'm not going to change. My guess is one-forty, give or take."

"What?" Stephanie asked, then quickly smiled. "Oh, the weight. That's what you think?"

"Yeah, how close am I?"

"I'm down to one hundred thirty-nine. Maybe you added the weight of the lunches and coffee?" Tobias laughed.

"No, I kind of figured that in. What's for lunch?" She pulled wrapped sandwiches from the bag and opened a container of coffee.

"Corned beef on rye with one of those big deli pickles you like, and coffee with a dab of half-and-half and one level teaspoon of sugar. How's that for a feast, your majesty!"

"Wonderful!" Tobias exclaimed, taking the sandwich from her. The aroma of the fresh rye bread and meat filled his nostrils, and smelled delicious.

"I'll be back in a moment," Stephanie said, taking the bag and a coffee as she opened the door to the healer's room. Tobias pulled several small pieces of crust from the bread for the pigeons and put them aside, then took a bite of the sandwich. It tasted wonderful. He smiled, congratulating himself on having won another game. Anthony had not realized he was blind.

Chapter Two

Tobias listened to the pigeons squabbling, then reached over and raised the window. The birds exploded into flight. The heavy aroma of bird excrement assailed his nostrils as he put some small pieces of bread crust on the sill and closed the window.

He stood and stepped carefully to begin his third perimeter walk around the room, to fix a three- dimensional image in his mind of his current surroundings. He felt the desk, then touched the walls and ran his hand along the chair rail as he progressed. He listened to every squeak of the floorboards as he completed the circuit, bumping into the chair that had been moved by Anthony. He adjusted it again, moving it farther back into the alcove and away from the top step, then returned to his desk, and listened to the sounds of the pigeons returning. He listened to them pecking at the bread crumbs, then Stephanie coming into the room and closing the healer's door softly behind her.

"He wouldn't eat, and yesterday he had about half a sandwich. He's looking worse and worse, Toby. We'd better get a doctor."

"You know what he's said about that, Steph. God's will and all that. He's not going to be with us much longer. I just wish he'd stopped the healing a long time ago…just goddamned stopped and retired! He's healed thousands of ungrateful bastards, and collectively they've killed him, as surely as if—"

"Toby, please…" Stephanie noted the catch in Tobias' voice. She stroked his arm gently, and in those few seconds she thought about him. He was unflappable, and except for the healer, almost unreachable emotionally. Tobias was absolutely and fanatically devoted to him. To everyone else, besides Stephanie, he was generally cynical, sarcastic, and abrasive. He especially had little patience for do-gooders and religious zealots of any kind.

"What did that man have, Toby?"

"A rash. I don't think he took much from the healer, if anything at all. A rash…can you honest to goddamned believe that?"

"Toby, you're too judgmental, especially when it comes to protecting the healer. The poor man may have been in agony for years. You have no way of knowing how bad it was for him."

The sound of the front door being opened brought their attention to the head of the stairs. Energetic footsteps followed and soon a comely young woman with long dark hair came into view. She was filled with the radiance of youth. Her bright smile exposed strong, white teeth as she walked briskly to Stephanie and embraced her.

"Hi, Audrey," Stephanie said as she returned the embrace. "I haven't had a chance to tell Tobias about you. I just got here myself."

"That's okay, Steph, I guess I'm a little early."

Tobias sat back in his chair and waited as they engaged in small talk. He had already calculated her weight and height as she walked upstairs, and also heard the swish of a skirt. This would be another volunteer to help Stephanie. There had been a string of them over the years, the tearful do-gooders that were filled with the Holy Spirit, determined to help the healer, and in turn God and mankind. Some lasted a few days, some a few weeks, and very few more than a couple of months.

They came in all varieties. Some were from the ranks of those that were healed, others friends and relatives of the healed, and some volunteers from local churches who heard of the healer. All had good intentions, but in the end the vicissitudes of life picked them off one by one. Family obligations, their jobs, other commitments, and just plain waning interest.

They would usually work enthusiastically for a few weeks, and then miss a day or two, then a week. Eventually they would all leave, with apologies. Tobias called them holy rockets who would blast off in a blaze of glory for God, only to fizzle out and fall away. None of their excuses ever set well with Tobias, no matter how rational.

The only steady beacon was Stephanie, who had served the healer faithfully for over twenty years, and the one before her seventeen years. Stephanie's husband had been cured by the healer and several years later, died in an automobile accident. After his cure Stephanie had volunteered to work for the healer to fulfill a vow to God for answering her prayers. She had never wavered in her commitment. Tobias turned his head up toward Audrey and smiled as he heard his name.

"Audrey, this is Tobias Barrows. Tobias, this is Audrey Sandler. She's volunteered to help the healer. She'll be taking Sissy's place. Sissy called and told me she's been promoted at work, and will be busier than ever working extra hours, so she just can't afford the time anymore. She said she was very, very sorry, and hopes you understand."

"Of course," Tobias replied, extending his hand and smiling generously for Stephanie's sake. He caught the mixed scent of soap, shampoo, and a light perfume as he felt the touch of smooth, young skin. He squeezed gently as she shook his hand lightly. Tobias heard an almost inaudible sigh of relief from Stephanie, who had expected a sarcastic response to the news. Audrey took those moments to study Tobias. She noted a thinnish man of medium height with a full head of graying auburn hair. His facial features were sharp and well-defined, including an aquiline nose. She could not see his eyes behind the tinted glasses.

"And what brings you to help the healer, Audrey?"

"I was away in college and heard that my aunt was cured by the healer. She raised me, Mr. Barrows, and is more than a mother to me. She's my dearest friend in the entire world. I'm just so grateful, and I wanted to do something for the healer. My aunt gave me Stephanie's name and phone number, so I called her to see if there was anything I could do. I really want to help. I've graduated and have a new job, but plenty of spare time."

"What was the nature of your aunt's problem?"

"Diabetes, very late stage. Her doctor gave her very little time, but now she's completely cured. She was here a few months ago. Her name is Nancy, Nancy Tupperman. Do you remember her?"

"No," Tobias lied, not wanting to get into an extended conversation. "We get so many people through here it's literally impossible to remember them all."

"I understand. Anyway, Stephanie tells me I'll be running errands for you and the healer. I'll leave my phone number, and also call you to check in. I'm just happy to have this opportunity."

"When can you start?"

"Tomorrow. My job is nine to five, and after that I have to prepare supper for my aunt and see to her needs. I would be available in the evenings and on weekends mostly."

"There won't be any evening work," Tobias replied. "I sleep on a cot in the healer's room. It would mainly be errands on the weekends, and even then, not every weekend."

"Sure, that would be fine, I can do that. Do you need anything now?"

"Yes, as a matter of fact I do. I need four or five folding chairs up here for groups, or family members that come in. We had some in the other place, but they were stolen from the truck during the move.

When you get the new chairs, place them on the other side of the room near the ones at the head of the stairs. I don't want any chairs placed beside my desk. I don't like people close to me. I can tell much more about someone from a distance."

"So Stephanie tells me. She said you have wonderful talents with your other senses."

"And so everyone tells me," Tobias replied dryly, and with some impatience in his voice. "You can get the chairs from any of the churches, but I'd contact the Elks club and places like that first. They all love to strut their Christianity, so you won't have any problem getting them to loan or donate. Please remember not to tell anyone where we're located. The only exception is someone you know or a member of your family that is in need of a cure. That's important, Audrey."

"All right, fine. Stephanie already told me all about that. Can I ask why? It sounds like a strange way to operate."

"It's very simple," Tobias answered, finally inured to having to explain it time after time after time. "If our location is known right away, crowds will show up immediately, and with that we invariably encounter problems. By problems I mean serious fights break out. Everyone is a judge of who should go ahead of whom. Even though we don't announce where we move to, they find us anyway. A few at first, and then it grows from there. By not announcing where we go, the healer can at least cure a few people before the crowds get out of hand and make it impossible to have order. Also, it gives the healer a chance to rest and recover."

"Okay, I'll make a few calls tonight. May I ask you how long you've worked for the healer?"

"Thirty-four years, since I was twenty-three years old." Audrey's face registered surprise. She had guessed his age was in the thirties.

"And Stephanie told me you're blind. Does it bother you to talk about it?"

"Yes, it does. Is there anything else, Audrey? I'd really like to get those chairs." Audrey ignored the annoyance in his voice.

"Can't the healer heal you?" Stephanie shook her head vigorously and tapped Audrey's forearm lightly to warn her off the subject. Tobias stood and extended his hand again.

"Nice to meet you, Audrey, I'm looking forward to working with you." Audrey took his hand, looking quizzically at Stephanie.

"Yes, yes…sure. I'll leave my phone number with Stephanie. Just call if you need anything." Tobias did not reply, and turned toward Stephanie.

"If you can stay, Steph, I'd like to catch a nap."

"Sure, go ahead Tobias."

"Do you need any more money for food and expenses?"

"No, Toby, I still have quite a bit," she answered. He then turned and entered the healer's room, closing the door behind him.

"I'm sorry," Audrey commented softly as the door closed. "I didn't know he was so sensitive about it."

"Don't fret about it," Stephanie replied, "it's just that that he's a very private person, and doesn't like being questioned personally. His manner can be pretty brusque, but he's a good man. You'll get used to him after awhile."

"I was just curious, Steph, that's all. Here he is blind, and he works for a man who heals. It was a natural question."

"I know it was, Audrey, I know. I should have told you more about Tobias. He has his eccentricities, and his manner can be very unfriendly. By the way, don't ever call him Toby. He lets me call him that, but for some reason he doesn't like others to do it. Whenever I'm with someone, I'm careful to call him Tobias." Audrey sighed at the complexity of it all and nodded her head. "As for his blindness, he's been sightless since he was six years old."

"My God," Audrey remarked, "the poor man. What happened to him?"

"He was living with his grandmother at the time. His parents were both drug addicts and one day they just left him without saying anything to anyone. The landlord found him a couple of days later wandering around in the apartment, crying his eyes out. Social services then got involved, found his grandmother, and brought him to her. She raised him. Anyway, his grandmother used to give him a paper bag with wet bread once in awhile to feed the pigeons in the park across from her home. As Tobias tells it, he was petting one and feeding it from his hand when he just suddenly lost his sight."

"So whatever caused it is incurable?" Audrey asked.

"They went the usual routes with doctors, but no one was able to pinpoint the cause."

"And I assume the healer tried but couldn't cure him?"

"Yeah, that's right. Toby was twenty-three then and had developed a deep faith in God. He was also working with other blind people, and doing a lot of good work. Someone heard of the healer and brought Toby there. Toby felt he was doing God's work, and that he was destined to come to the healer at that point. He looked forward to getting his sight back, but didn't get cured obviously. You have to realize, Audrey, this healer is very unique. He heals like Christ did. Cures are affected immediately, and Toby had had high expectations. Anyway, as Toby puts it, all bets were off after that. He blamed God, or the lack thereof, and he's stubbornly refused to try again. God had his chance, as he put it.

"And he can't stand those he calls Jesus freaks, so be careful talking about your faith. And while we're on that subject, don't quote Bible to him if you're so inclined. He's very well read, chapter and verse, and he'll run circles around you." Audrey sighed again, obviously confused, but somehow oddly attracted to the mysteriousness of it all.

"So why does he work for the healer?"

"Because he loves the man, plain and simple. Toby says he has the purest heart of any human being he has ever met. He describes him as a saint who does what he does out of his love for mankind, not to get to heaven. Toby says his faith is in the healer, and not in anyone else, nor any God of any sort."

"This is so bizarre," Audrey commented, shaking her head.

"I agree," Stephanie replied, "but the fact of the matter is that he would literally die for the healer, and God help anyone who would ever attempt to harm him." Audrey had one more small question she wanted answered.

"Steph, I noticed his right pinky finger is distorted. It has a hooked appearance. Couldn't…"

"You are observant!" Stephanie chuckled. "He caught his finger in a car door when he was a child and broke it. His parents didn't feel the need to take him to a doctor, especially since they needed drug money, and that's the way it healed. And before you ask the question, no, he won't let the healer correct that either."

Before Audrey could reply, the sound of the door opening downstairs caught their attention. The door closed, followed by a confusion of noises. Audrey furrowed her brows. "What's going on down there?"

"There are two people, I think," Stephanie replied. "I think one has a cane. Not good news."

Tobias

Stephanie went to the head of the stairs and confirmed her observation. "Do you need any help down there?" she called. A young woman answered, and replied they were fine. Their progress was slow, but several minutes later an older man with a cane, accompanied by an attractive young woman, emerged at the top of the stairs. Stephanie gestured for the old man to sit in a chair, then extended her hand to the young woman.

"Are you the healer?" asked the woman.

"No," Stephanie answered, "I'm a volunteer. I help out with chores and such. The healer is in another room. The woman glanced at Audrey, then shifted her attention back to Stephanie and began to speak rapidly.

"My name is Janine. This is my great grandfather, Corey. We've never been to a faith healer before, so I'm not sure what we do. I hope you can help him. I know he's old, but we don't want to lose him. I hope there's no age limitation. Please, don't send us away. Do we need to make an appointment? Is it okay to just come here like this? I'm so sorry to intrude, but I…"

"Everything's fine, Janine, but the greeter is sleeping right now, and so is the healer. Can you return in an hour? I hate to ask you to come back, but he needs the rest. And please forgive me, I'm so sorry, I should have thought to tell you that before your grandfather climbed these stairs." The woman looked confused, then annoyed, then resigned. She nodded her assent, helped Corey to his feet, and together they wended their way down the stairs and out of the building.

Philip Birmingham

Chapter Three

Tobias awoke to Stephanie's gentle nudging. He rolled over, sat up on the cot and rubbed his eyes. She picked up his tinted glasses from the nightstand and touched them to his hand.

"Time to get up, Toby. There's some people who'll be coming back. They were here before, but I sent them away for awhile."

She walked across the room to the healer. She looked down compassionately at his slender frame. He was lying on his right side, his right arm, shoulder, and both legs awkwardly contorted. He was a small man in his mid-fifties, and at least fifty pounds underweight. She stroked his arm gently and smiled as he opened his eyes. He returned the smile. "Please," she said softly, "it's time to stop. You need to be somewhere you can get care. You can come to my house, I have plenty of room. Please, you've given so much...so much. Please, let me take care of you and spend your last days resting and relaxing. I'll spoil you with wonderful food, and all the care you need. It would be an honor...an honor. God, please..."

He smiled steadily at her and slowly shook his head as he reached for her hand. She took it in her own. It was cold. She gently massaged it, feeling the bones that were barely covered by skin. It was clear from his eyes that he had made up his mind to end his life right where he was. She heard Tobias leave the room. She patted the healer's hand, then turned and also left the room. Tobias was at his desk.

"He looks so bad, Toby. I wonder if we shouldn't just take the bull by the horns and get a doctor up here." Tobias shook his head vigorously.

"No, no, no, I've told you...absolutely not! I've had more than one long discussion with him about this. This is what he wants. He knows that all the healings diminish him, and he's well aware that he's dying. I've pleaded with him to reconsider, and he's pleaded with me to respect his wishes, and that's what I'm doing. You're one of my closest friends, Steph, and I can count those on the fingers of one hand. Please, don't meddle in this. I know how frustrating it is for you, but it's no less frustrating for me."

"Okay," she replied, almost in a whisper. "I won't mention it again, Toby, but let's agree we don't move again no matter what. It's too traumatic for him." Tobias nodded his head in assent. He then heard a large sigh from her, followed by the downstairs door opening. He listened for a few seconds.

"Two people, one is a male with a cane. I think the other one is a woman."

"Oh, yes...yes, those are the people I told you about. They were here earlier. Her name is Janine, but I've forgotten her grandfather's name." Stephanie walked to the head of the stairs and smiled as she watched the couple. She offered help, which was accepted this time, and Stephanie then went downstairs to meet them. Their progress was still exceedingly slow, and when they finally reached the head of the stairs, Stephanie helped them to the chairs, then turned to Tobias.

"Goodbye, Tobias, I'll see you around supper time." Tobias smiled and waved at her.

"Are you the healer?" Janine asked.

"No, my name is Tobias. I greet all those who want to see the healer." He observed a young female voice, as well as the underlying current of desperation in her voice. "What is the nature of your problem?"

"I'm here about my great-grandfather," she replied, gesturing toward the old man. "His name is Corey. He has a heart condition, and the doctor wants him in hospice as soon as possible. The doctor said it would be a matter of weeks. As you can see, he's very old, and I know that one day we're going to lose him anyway, but he's well loved by his family, and if it's possible we want him to have a few more years. I have some medical papers with me. I didn't know if you would need them. I didn't know what to bring." Her voice began to break with emotion. "Please, I know he's old, but he..."

"You need not bring anything," Tobias answered. "I'm sorry he has to climb up all those stairs. It sounds like he should be in a wheelchair. Can your grandfather speak?" Tobias had noted the man's labored breathing during his conversation with Janine.

"Yes," the old men replied slowly, "but please give me a few moments. I need to catch my breath."

"Take all the time you need, Corey. Tell me, Janine, how did you find us?"

"One of the members of our church. She said she thought the healer had moved here, but wasn't sure. I don't know how she knew. Will you be able to help us?"

Tobias winced inwardly, knowing the old man's condition was serious, and the toll it would take on the healer. He was greatly tempted to tell Janine that it was time to let go, that the old man had lived a long and apparently fruitful life, and to just let nature take its course. But he had given his word. No one would ever be refused.

"I don't know, Janine. I never know the outcome until people come out of that room behind me. Even then, sometimes…"

"Sir?" the old man interrupted.

"Yes, Corey?"

"I really didn't want to come here. I'm ninety-three years old, and I've had a blessed life. A wonderful wife, wonderful children, grandchildren and great-grandchildren. I don't want to leave them, but I know there are people much worse off than I am who need healing. My family pestered me to come here and I finally gave in, but now I realize I have no right to ask for more. I'm sorry, I shouldn't—".

"Grandpa, please," Janine interrupted. "Please let the healer see you." She was close to tears, and looked toward Tobias imploringly. "My grandmother died 3 years ago, and he's all alone. We all visit him regularly."

Tobias picked up nuances in the old man's voice that told him the he was close to tears as well. Tobias liked what he heard from him, not just the content, but the sincerity in his voice, and Tobias was an expert in that regard.

"She's right, Corey. By all means, go in and see the healer." Tobias then recited his canned speech about the healer's condition and how to approach him. He left out that any cure would be detrimental to the healer.

He heard them rise, the old man shuffling while he leaned on Janine for support. As they passed, Janine whispered "Thank you." As the door shut, Tobias closed his eyes and leaned back in his chair. If there was a cure, there would sure as hell be a price to pay. Tobias wondered about God. How could He be real and allow all of this pain and suffering to the healer? What was the point? The pigeons cooing gave background noises to his thoughts. He felt the desk for any crumbs that he might have missed. There were none. After several minutes passed, he heard the door open downstairs. Then the door closed and there was silence. This was not an unusual event, as some backed out at the last moment.

Several minutes passed before the door behind him opened. Tobias' senses came to high alert. Janine was crying as she and the old man emerged from the room. The old man's steps were pronounced and energetic as he crossed the room. There was no shuffling. Janine walked back stood in front of the desk. He resisted the urge to get up and check on the healer.

"I assume it went well," Tobias asked. There was no reply. "Janine?" Janine collapsed to her knees and lowered her head on the desk, sobbing. He reached out and patted her arm.

"He's cured. He said he felt it surge through his body. He felt pains in his chest, but they quickly went away, and he said he knew he was cured. He's cured…he's cured. God, thank you…thank you, God…thank you." There was the sound of snuffling, and tissues being taken from the box of Kleenex on his desk as she brought herself under control and stood. "I meant to ask the cost, but I forgot. How much is it?"

"Nothing," Tobias answered.

"Nothing? My God, nothing? A donation then." He heard a small purse open and the sound of money being taken out. "There's seventy-three dollars, but I have more in my savings account. I'll be back with it as soon as I can. I have seven hundred…"

"There's no need for that, Janine. We have plenty of donations and we're doing just fine. What kind of work do you do?" There was a hesitation. She fumbled in her purse, reached for more tissues from the box, then blew her nose.

"I was laid off at work, but I have an interview Monday. Please, I want to donate something." Tobias sensed her need.

"Very well, the usual donation is twenty-five dollars. That will be just fine." He felt money touch the side of his finger as she pushed it toward him. She looked at him quizzically.

"Please, that's not enough. Let me get more and return."

"No," Tobias said, firmly. "If we were in need, I would tell you. Go, and take your grandfather for a stroll. It's a beautiful day." He heard her turn and take two steps. She turned back.

"Tobias?"

"Yes?"

"Are you…I don't mean to be personal, but are you…"

"Yes, I'm blind."

"I didn't realize it until you reached for the money." Tobias smiled and shrugged his shoulders. "Can't you be…"

"It's a long story, Janine, and not something I want to talk about. Please, take your grandfather and leave. I'm happy he was cured." Janine returned to the head of the stairs as the old man stood.

"Thank you," the man said. The tone and liquid sounds of his voice said it all.

"You're welcome," Tobias replied. "You're very, very welcome, Corey."

As they descended, Tobias stood and opened the door behind him and entered.

Philip Birmingham

Chapter Four

Tobias walked to the healer and sat down. The healer opened his eyes and smiled, then extended his hand. Tobias felt the touch and took it in his own. It was cold, as he expected.

"I know that one took its toll. How bad is it?"

"I'm fine, Tobias," came the raspy reply. "It wasn't that bad." Then, anticipating the next question, "Please, please, no more urging me to get help. Please tell that to Stephanie again. I know I'm dying, and I've made my peace with God. Please, Tobias, please. I can't stand any more of it." He heard the healer's voice trail off as he ran out of breath.

"God can go pound salt," Tobias replied in a harsh whisper. "Fine, I won't say a single word anymore, but I think that you're very close to death. Stephanie says you look terrible, and I can feel a difference in you after that last man that you healed." The healer gently squeezed Tobias' hand and took a breath.

"I won't let you blame God, Tobias. You know how I feel. I know I'm close, and I want you to do something for me." Tobias released his hand quickly and sat up straight.

"You're right, you're right, I should respect your wishes. I give you my solemn promise, I won't mention it again, and I won't insult your God again. I know it grieves you when I do that. I'm sorry, I'm just so frustrated to think of you like this. It was an outburst, that's all."

"Very well, my cherished friend," the healer answered, "then we won't speak of it again. You've been with me many years, Tobias. You've sacrificed your life and all you could be for me. To me that is a greater love than dying for someone. I have thanked you many times before, and I thank you again. You've been my rock, my anchor. Now, I would ask yet another favor."

"No," Tobias answered quickly, "because I know what it is, and I refuse to do it."

"Please, let me try again." There was urgency in the voice.

"No. Your God had his chance. I won't make another attempt. I'll respect your wishes for you to die healing a lot of smelly, whiny, ungrateful people, but you need to respect mine." Tobias heard a small sigh.

"Very well, I'll respect your wishes as well." Tobias was angry at the injustice of it all. He inwardly raged at a God he did not believe in that would permit the healer to suffer like this.

"That first man that you healed this morning. Do you know what his problem was? Did you ask him? Did you know that all he had was a rash? A goddamn rash! Why don't you let me determine who really needs you, and who doesn't?" An exasperated sound escaped the healer.

"Yes…yes, I know. When I took his hand I could sense that his problem was minor. You're too judgmental, Tobias. The man was greatly affected emotionally, and he may go on to pledge his service to mankind, and maybe do great things. You have no way of knowing. The healing was not wasted. I don't think it ever is. You don't know the man, and you don't know why God brought him here." Then, after a pause, he smiled and added, "He might even have been an angel, Tobias." Tobias stood.

"Yeah, yeah, I know the Bible quote. Many have entertained angels unawares," Tobias snapped. "Don't quote Saint Paul to me, I don't believe in him either. But you're right, I won't fight you anymore. You're right, you're right." Tobias turned and left the room.

He had no more than seated himself when he heard the downstairs door open and the sound of someone taking the stairs two at a time. A man dressed in a suit and tie appeared at the head of the stairs and strode toward Tobias' desk, ignoring the fact that there was no chair there. Tobias felt a tinge of fear in his stomach. The stride signaled a heavy-set man on a mission of urgency. He braced for the worst. The man put his hands on the desk and leaned forward, bringing his face very close to Tobias. He could feel the heat from it, along with the man's breath and the smell of perspiration.

"Are you the so-called healer?" Tobias' fear was replaced by anger.

"No, and I'd appreciate it if you would step back away from me. You're too close…you're invading my personal space, and you don't smell very good." The man chuckled and stood erect.

"Fine, fine. Where's the famous healer. I want to talk to him, right away."

"Who are you, and why do you want to see him? What's the nature of your problem?"

"Reverend Widmer. I'm the pastor at United Church of God. Now, who in God's name are you?"

"My name is Tobias. I work for the healer. Why are you…"

"I said I need to see the one that does the healing…right away."

"I heard what you said, but I still need the reason you're here, Reverend." The man began pacing.

"Very well, I usually don't deal with subordinates, but I'll make an exception. One of my parishioners came to me today and said she heard of your healer, and told me where he was located. She asked my advice about seeing him."

"What's the nature of her problem?"

"It's her daughter, but that's none of your business. I told her about the Biblical injunction against false prophets, and that she should—"

"The healer is not a prophet, Reverend, he's a healer."

"Oh, and who does he heal in the name of? Does he believe in God, and does he accept Jesus Christ as his personal Savior? What faith does he hold to? Is he a Christian? Is he—"

"Stop right there Reverend. I know he believes in God, and to my knowledge when he heals he does it silently, and does not invoke the name of any deity. He does attribute his gift to God. That I do know, and that is all you need to know. Personally, I don't believe in God, or Jesus Christ for that matter. The rest of it is none of your business." The man paced back and forth again several times.

"That's blasphemy!"

"No it isn't. Blasphemy is classically defined as a verbal insult against God, and I just informed you I don't believe in God.

"Whatever…I'm entitled to check him out. It's my duty and obligation. This woman is part of my flock, and I take the job of shepherd very seriously. It's my mission to check his credentials. This woman's daughter has renal disease, and for all I know your man performs one of those so-called surgeries where he extracts diseased organs magically through the skin, and which has already been debunked as nothing more than secreted chicken guts." Tobias remained calm.

"Let me explain the procedure to you, Reverend, it's—"

"I don't need to hear a lot of mumbo-jumbo from any front man. Let me see him and question him, then I'll be the one—"

Philip Birmingham

Tobias suddenly realized how vulnerable the situation was. If the man bulled his way into the healer's room, there was nothing he could do to stop him. Tobias prepared himself to try at all costs.

"Reverend Widmer, the healer is not here just yet. He may not be in until tomorrow. As for what he does, his method is just to hold the person's hand for a few minutes. That's all there is to it."

"And then he keeps them coming back for more visits? Is that the way it works? How much are the visits?"

"I understand your skepticism, but—"

"I said how many visits?"

"He sees a person once," Tobias replied. "There is no cost, other than a donation if the person is so inclined."

"Great, and I'm sure everyone gets talked into a sizeable gift. Does he file taxes? Is he affiliated with any church? I think maybe you're hiding plenty. Perhaps the police should pay you a visit."

"Perhaps you're right, Reverend. There's the phone," Tobias answered, gesturing toward it. The reverend glared at him.

"Mind taking those glasses off? I can't see your eyes. A person's eyes tell me a lot about their soul."

"Yes, I do mind taking my glasses off."

"Suit yourself. I guess I'll be telling my parishioner that I've checked the healer out, and in my opinion your so-called healer is nothing more than a false prophet. No one can heal miraculously but our Lord and Savior, Jesus Christ, and only He—" Tobias stood and raised his voice slightly.

"Stop!" he said. "First, Rev, let me explain that a prophet, as classically defined and used in the Bible, speaks the words of God, and may or may not tell the future, and may or may not have the ability to heal. You can spot a potential one by the words, 'Thus says the Lord.' Secondly, you're profoundly wrong about others not having the ability to heal. Remember our beloved Saint Peter, after Christ died, healing a man? And are you familiar with Saint Paul's dissertation in Corinthians one, verse twelve, on the diversity of gifts? One of those gifts was, and I quote, 'gifts of healing by that one Spirit, and to another miraculous powers,' and so forth." The minister stepped back from the desk.

"I see you're apparently well-versed in your Bible." Tobias' calm reply belied the content of his words.

"And I see you're apparently not, you arrogant, self-righteous, self-important ass," Tobias calmly replied. "I'd appreciate it if you'd leave, Widmer. In my opinion you're a small-minded man who'll end up denying your parishioner a chance to be healed. And for that matter, what are your credentials? Where did you get your theology training…at Wal-Mart? So be it, but at the very least take the time to learn your own Bible. It's part of your job, and an obligation as you put it, to your so-called flock. Personally, I think you're ignorance is blatantly clear, and I think you're an embarrassment to all Christian clergy. And as for organized religion of any kind, I think they and you are participants in a sham."

"Blasphemy, plain and simple!" Widmer shot back. By then Tobias was in full calm mode, knowing it was an irritation to the man.

"Your accusation is in error, as I pointed out before. Blasphemy is a verbal insult to God, Reverend, and nothing I said fits that category."

"Go to Hell!" Widmer stormed, turning and walking to the head of the stairs.

"Is that what Jesus would say?" Tobias called after him. He listened to the heavy retreating steps, the pause as the door was yanked open, and then slammed shut.

Tobias leaned back and took a deep breath, then reached into the desk drawer and extracted a small tape recorder.

"Note to Stephanie. Steph, I had an episode today that put me in fear for the healer. I'll tell you about it later. Please look into getting permission from the landlord to put a lock on the door to the back room, and a coded key pad to operate it from my desk, so I can lock and unlock the door electronically. We need something that can be taken with us from place to place." Then, after a pause, "On second thought, we agreed this was the last move. Let's just ask the landlord if it's okay to install some kind of security device."

Philip Birmingham

Chapter Five

A full hour passed, during which Tobias paced about the room. Every few minutes his thoughts came to the healer, and his imminent death. Would it be today? Tomorrow? He knew it was close, and he once again failed to put it out of his mind. *What will I do? I don't want to move to Idaho and live with my brother, but I may have no choice.* Stephanie had broached the subject several times, offering to take Tobias into her home, but Tobias did not like charity, or being a burden to anyone else. Yet, she was insistent and seemed sincere, and he reasoned it might do temporarily until things worked themselves out. He decided his response would depend on what he could contribute.

The door opening downstairs sent him back to his desk. He heard a cane. He extracted the recorder and put it on the desk to remind himself to make another note for Stephanie. He decided that there would be no more second floor locations, as he always anguished when he heard people laboring up the stairs. Then he remembered that this was the last location.

He listened carefully to the person's ascent. Slight build, steps like a man. The cane sounded different, tapping the wall and stairs as it progressed. A blind man. When the stranger was halfway up the stairs the door opened again, and he heard another man's voice.

"Charlie…wait. Just stay put and I'll help ya up." Then the sound of energetic steps. When he caught up to Charlie, both men continued slowly, finally emerging at the head of the stairs.

"Here, Charlie, take a seat here. Feel it? There, that's it." The man looked at Tobias. "Hi, you the guy that does the healing thing?"

"No, I'm Tobias. I work for the healer. Your friend is apparently blind, correct?" He heard the man sit down.

"Yeah, yeah he's blind. This is my friend Charlie."

"Hi Tobias," Charlie added, "You sound like you're all the way across the room. Why are we sitting here?" Tobias liked his read on their voices immediately.

"I just prefer to interview people at a distance. For some reason I'm more comfortable that way. You can both bring your chairs over here if it bothers you."

"Nah, we're fine," the other man replied. "I'm Quincy. Charlie and I live on the streets together. I guess ya can tell by our crappy clothes." Tobias had already detected the mingled odors of body sweat and dirty apparel emanating from them or, as someone had once dubbed it, 'the odor of sanctity.' There was a certain combined odor to street people.

"How did you find us?" Tobias asked. Quincy answered.

"We was both on the street in fronta' the buildin', panhandlin', and this woman comes out with this old guy. She's like all cryin' an talkin' a mile a minute about how her grandfather got cured, and I figured she might be good for a buck or two. She gave us each ten bucks and hugged us, and then told us about her grandfather. Jesus H. Christ, ain't nobody ever hugged me and Charlie in years. Anyways, so me and Charlie discussed it and decided to give it a shot. I know we're dirty, and we're bums and all that, but…"

"Don't worry about it, Quincy, you're welcome here. How old are you, Charlie?"

"I'm about fifty, I guess. Not really sure. I been on the streets a long time. I lived with relations and in foster homes a lot, and my birthday got confused somewhere along the way."

"How long have you been blind?"

"Ever since we both got mugged in the park," Quincy interrupted. "A gang of kids beat the hell outa' us. They hit us with baseball bats. I'm talkin' young kids… teenagers. Christ Almighty, we didn't do a goddamn thing to 'em…nuthin'. Charlie here got a broken nose and a concussion, and they broke his ribs and one of his kneecaps, too. They hit me a coupla times right in the frickin' head and I went out like a light. Charlie got the worst of it. He was in a coma for a coupla' days, and ended up blind. Blind as a bat…blind as a bat. Jesus H. Christ."

"How long ago was that?"

"About a year ago," Quincy replied. "They lemme me outa the hospital the same day, then Charlie three days later. He shoulda stayed there longer, but they knew we couldn't pay nuthin'. Bastards. Charlie's been blind as a bat ever since…blind as a bat. They whacked him in the head a lot. Jesus…Jesus Christ, his face looked like hamburger. Hey, at least you ate good for a coupla' days, right Charlie? They let me visit him, and Charlie snuck me soma' his hospital food."

"Why did they beat you up like that?" Tobias asked. "You didn't have any money, did you?"

"Nah, they wuz just out for some laughs. That kinda stuff has happened before, but not that bad. I think these kids wanted ta kill us though, I mean, the way they was talkin' and yellin', and eggin' each other on, but I think they got scared and changed their minds. They wuz pretty well dressed. One of 'em was even takin' movies. We stopped at the cops' station a coupla' weeks later to find out if they were investigatin' it, but they weren't, and they told us to get the hell outa' the station, or they'd lock us up for vagrancy. Hell, once some kids wanted to pay us to fight each other, but we didn't. What's the difference anyway? If they catch 'em, their parents would jus' get a lawyer an get'em off. It's not like Charlie's gonna get his sight back. Sometimes we used to get day work, but now Charlie can't even do that no more."

Tobias made his prefatory remarks about the healer, then both men walked to the door and entered. Tobias' attention went to the window and the cooing sounds. He felt sorry for both men. There was no animosity in their voices, just a calm acceptance of their lot in life, and getting on with whatever destiny threw at them. He had long ago refrained from judging anyone in those circumstances. He made a mental note to give them each twenty dollars from the desk.

A full five minutes passed before the door opened and the men walked out. He didn't like what he heard. Charlie was still tapping the floor in all directions with his cane.

"How did it go, Charlie?"

"Nuthin'," Quincy replied. That's okay, though, ain't it Charlie? It was worth a shot...what the hell. Christ, Charlie, I shouldna' talked ya into it." Quincy then directed his comments to Tobias. "The healer guy looks like he's in bad shape, you prob'ly oughta get him to a doctor. That's prob'ly why he couldn't fix Charlie." Charlie made no comments.

"I'm sorry," Tobias replied.

"We owe anything?" Charlie asked. "All we got is twenty bucks between us and some change. I mean, he didn't get healed or nothin', so do we still halfta pay?" Tobias opened the desk and extracted a cigar box.

"No, no charge. In fact, here, here's some money." Tobias opened the box and pushed it toward them. "Take forty dollars and leave the rest." There was a pause.

"Are you blind?" Quincy asked.

"Yes, I am. Don't take any more than forty dollars, Quincy, okay?"

"No, okay, I won't, honest ta God. Jeez, thanks, Toby, thanks." Tobias heard Quincy pick up the bills and sort them, then drop the remainder back in the box. "Anything me and Charlie can do for you guys? I could sweep up and stuff like that. You wouldn't have to pay me nuthin' more."

"No," Tobias replied. "Good luck to both of you."

"Okay. So long, Toby. C'mon Charlie, we're eatin' like kings tonight. Both men crossed the room and started downstairs. He listened to the sounds of cane tapping as they descended. About halfway down, they stopped.

"Holy crap, Quince! Holy shit!" Tobias smiled. "Quince…Oh, Christ, Quince…Christ Almighty."

"What's it, Charlie, whatsamatter?"

"My freakin' sight is comin' back. Holy crap, Quince, I can see you! It's gettin' better by the second. Jesus, Mary, and Joseph, Quince! Jesus, Quince…Jesus!" There was a heavy thumping sound as Charlie sat down abruptly on the stairs.

The babbling went on non-stop for several minutes, then Charley came back up the stairs and let loose with a profusion of garbled thanks for several minutes. Quincey appeared shortly afterward, followed by both of them raving excitedly. Finally they left, and Tobias heard the downstairs door close.

He stood and walked into the back room and sat down beside the healer, and listened intensely to the healer's breathing.

"Want me to call it a day, and send the rest away?"

"No, Tobias, don't do that," came the hoarse reply. "Please, please don't do that." Tobias stroked the healer's hand. Somehow it seemed even colder than before. He felt for the uneaten sandwich on the small stand beside the healer.

"Please, eat something. Okay?" The healer nodded and raised his hand. Tobias felt it and helped him sit upright and handed him the sandwich. The bread felt stale. "Can I get you something else? How about some water? That coffee's cold by now. I can reheat it on the hot plate." The healer took Tobias' hand and held it to his cheek, then shook his head. Tobias listened to him slowly chew the sandwich. He doubted he would live through the day, much less the week. He felt urged to offer medical help again, but honored his word and held his tongue. Then he stood and walked out of the room.

Tobias

He walked immediately to the window, knelt on one knee, and cocked his head to the side. The pigeons were gone. He sat down at the desk. He reasoned that he needed to stop obsessing about the healer, to put it out of his mind. He reasoned it was out of his control, and he had to accept that. He leaned back in the chair and faced up toward the ceiling.

"Hey, big guy, where are you? You've got a genuine saint in that back room, and you're letting his ass rot. Nice going…nice going. You know he believes in you? I don't. If you're really there, strike me dead with a lightning bolt. Do something! Why do you have to let him die with pain? What's the point? He's the purest, sweetest human being I've ever encountered." Tobias let out a loud sigh. "I'd probably be better off calling that asshole minister that was here. Maybe he could make me feel better by telling me that God works in mysterious ways, and all that bullshit cop-out pious religious pablum. There's always a stock answer for why God doesn't respond, always some off-the-wall reason someone can back into. And when there's a favorable and coincidental outcome, you get the credit, don't you? Someone has a close shave with death…God was with me…it's a miracle…God must be sparing me for something special." Tobias waved a dismissive hand at the ceiling. "Out of lightning bolts, big guy? And for that matter, why am I talking to the figment of everyone's collective imagination?"

Tobias heard the pigeons returning and activity downstairs at the same time. He took a deep breath. *Be something minor, please…* Then, suddenly, it flashed across his mind that something serious might be just the thing. It might be the silver bullet that would end the healer's suffering.

Philip Birmingham

Chapter Six

The next hour brought two more seekers, both with minor ailments. One donated ten dollars, and the other fifty dollars. The more generous donor offered voluntary services, which Tobias declined. That was followed by two people, both women, squabbling by the downstairs door about who got there first, and who was most deserving. They ended up shouting insults at each other and then, for some inexplicable reason, both of them left without coming upstairs.

Although he could perceive no light whatsoever, Tobias knew the sun was setting. This was due to a combination of things. First, his internal clock, which gave him an accurate grasp of the passage of time. Other factors were his increasing appetite for food, changes in the air temperature, the diminishing sounds of everyday commerce around him and, most important, a simple sixth sense that light was fading. This ability he had demonstrated to friends in a closed room with no windows.

Noises reached him from downstairs. He smelled food at the same time he recognized Stephanie's footsteps. She reached the head of the stairs and strode to his desk, where the usual greetings were exchanged. More familiar sounds of plastic bags and paper cups.

"Of course you know what it is, don't you?" Stephanie remarked.

"Mac and cheese."

"How the heck can you tell that from closed plastic containers?"

"The odor is on your clothes. I can also smell soap, your perfume, and bleach." Stephanie shook her head incredulously. She placed his supper in front of him and nudged his hand, then made up a plate for the healer.

"How is he doing? Any real bad ones?"

"He's about the same," Tobias answered, "and no, there haven't been any really bad ones." He then told her about the incident with the minister, and asked her to check on getting some type of security device for the door. Following that she went into the healer's room. Several minutes later she returned.

"He ate pretty well," she remarked. "I think he looks a little better then he did this morning. I know he loves mac and cheese, so that's why I made it."

"Good," Tobias replied. "Did you lock the downstairs door, Steph? I think we're through for today."

"Yes, yes, I did. I'll double-check when I leave."

"He's really an utterly unique human being, isn't he," Tobias remarked, gesturing to the room behind.

"I've never ever heard or seen the likes of him, Toby."

"Steph, I've been witness to instant cures on bone cancers. New bone actually replacing diseased bone. I've witnessed cures to people with all types of ailments. Bones actually twisting and bending themselves back into position while the disabled are here. It happens immediately, and it never fails to stun and amaze me. I've never heard of any healer having that dramatic a power. And his cure rate is high, probably in the ninetieth percentile."

"It has to come from God, Tobias. I know you don't want to hear that, but these cures are beyond the natural…far beyond. They are miraculous. Even the petty little illnesses are all noteworthy. I'll never believe it doesn't come from God."

"There are phenomenal things in this world, Steph, and phenomenal people with phenomenal talents, and all explainable. Many of them make no claim to God whatsoever."

"I don't want to argue with you, Toby, but you're biased. You didn't get your sight back, and then immediately you became an atheist, or whatever term you use. If you had been cured, you would have believed. You know that's true, Toby." She expected an outburst, and was surprised at the calm reply.

"It's a valid point, Steph, but you don't know me. I'm as convinced as I can be that there is no God…none whatsoever. It's easier to believe that certain people have phenomenal powers than to believe in a God." She did not reply or rise to the challenge, and Tobias listened to the sounds she made gathering up her belongings. She called back from the head of the stairs.

"I'll be back tomorrow with some breakfast, Toby. Call me if you need anything. No hard feelings, okay?"

"Okay," Tobias answered, smiling at her. "No hard feelings." He listened to her footsteps as she left, then the door close and lock. He ate his supper, saving part of a roll for the pigeons, then went in to check on healer. When he sat, he felt the healer's hand touch his knee. He took the hand and held it.

"How are you feeling? Do you need anything?"

"Help me up, Tobias, I need to go to the bathroom." Tobias helped him to and his feet, and listened to him shuffle painfully across the room to the bathroom door. Several minutes later the healer returned and sat down on the bed.

"Tobias...I don't have much time left. You know that."

"Yes, of course, I know that...of course." Tobias knew what was coming.

"You've served me for years, both you and Stephanie, and I only wish there was something to leave you, to repay both of you for all you've done."

"We've talked about this before. I don't want anything, and neither does Steph."

"I'm begging you, Tobias, begging you. Please let me try once more, while I still have breath in me."

"No, I made a vow to myself, and I intend to keep it. I have carried out your wishes without question, and you need to respect mine."

"Why?"

"You know why. We've discussed this many times."

"It's just plain stubbornness, Tobias. You blame a God that you don't believe in. If he doesn't exist, then what that amounts to is that you don't believe in me."

"Don't skew it that way. You know I believe in you. I've witnessed what you do every day. You're a genuine phenomenon. No healer in the entire history of the world has been able to do the things that you do. It's palpable, don't you see? It can be demonstrated over and over. It doesn't even require faith. You deliver, consistently."

"It is my dying wish."

"No, don't even think about throwing that guilt trip on me."

"I do, Tobias. I ask you to let me try once more, just once more. It will cost you nothing but the breaking of a vow to yourself, a vow that was foolish and prideful, and one you never should have made in the first place. I love you, Tobias, but your vow is childish stubbornness."

Tobias breathed a heavy sigh, but did not reply. The healer waited while several moments of awkward silence followed. Tobias rose and walked toward the door. "Tobias...please...please. Once more, and I will never ask you again. Please do this for me." Tobias stopped, his hand on the doorknob, then turned his head in the healer's direction. "Please, Tobias, please."

"Very well. I will not have it on my mind that I refused a friend his dying wish. Promise me that after you try, there will be no more talk of this…ever. I want your promise, and make it a solemn one."

"I so promise," the healer replied. He reached for Tobias' hand. "I know you can't see, but close your eyes, Tobias. Please give me all the faith you can, all that you can muster." Tobias nodded his assent and closed his eyes. The healer reached for his other hand. Tobias felt the healer's hands gradually tightening on his own.

Several seconds passed, during which Tobias thought he felt something stirring within him. He dared to have the merest hope for the possibility of what could be. He allowed himself to envision an amorphous spiritual form. A God, for want of a better term. He felt a small but growing expectation…hope. More seconds passed, which turned into a minute.

"Tobias…is anything…?"

"No, nothing…nothing whatsoever." Tobias pulled his hands free and walked to the door. The healer sighed, hung his head and began to weep. A minute later, he laid painfully back on the bed and rolled to his side.

Tobias sat at his desk and listened to the pigeons. He opened the desk drawer and removed a book of fiction written in Braille, and began scanning the pages with his fingertips. Several minutes later, he closed the book and fought back tears, inwardly chiding himself for even daring to hope. Wiping his eyes with his sleeve, he went to the window and dropped the crumbs on the sill for the pigeons to find in the morning, then went to make tea for himself and the healer.

The noises of street waned with each passing hour, until only the occasional sound broke the quiet of the night. A car horn every so often, or the muffled voices of the night denizens of the city, those people who just seemed to appear in the darkened streets like nocturnal animals. He went into the small bathroom and brushed his teeth, then lay on his cot. Thoughts of the day went through his mind, then bizarre shapes and faces floated in his mind until he finally succumbed to the urge to sleep. Tomorrow was another day.

Chapter Seven

Morning noises and the occasional car horn from the street below awakened Tobias. He laid still and listened carefully. The healer was breathing rhythmically. Tobias quietly rose from the cot, went into the bathroom, and attended to his morning ritual. Following that, he quietly left the room and went to his desk. He guessed the time to be about seven o'clock. The pigeons were already waiting on the sill when he reached his desk. He listened for several moments and concluded a fifth pigeon had joined the others. Twenty minutes later he heard the familiar key in the lock downstairs. As soon as Stephanie entered the hallway and closed the door, he smelled the coffee. He felt his stomach react. These sounds and aromas were the highlights of his day.

Stephanie was in a good mood, as usual, and chatted as she sorted out the breakfast. She had called the landlord and had received permission to do whatever was necessary to ensure the healer's safety. She planned a trip to the hardware store to see if something could be donated. To Tobias' delight, she had brought several extra slices of bread for his pigeons.

"I'm going to leave now, Toby, and I might be a little late for lunch. I have some things to do. I'll let you know how I make out with a lock for the door. Oh, and before I forget, Audrey got some chairs and she'll drop them by later on. What else? Oh, yes, there's a man downstairs pacing around on the sidewalk. I think he's working up the courage to come up here. He's well dressed, and he doesn't appear to be disabled in any way. I thought I'd let you know." With that she said her goodbye and left.

Tobias took one of the bread slices and broke it into pieces, opened the window, and spread them on the sill. The rest he set aside to stale and harden. When he closed the window and turned back to his desk, he smiled at the flurry of wings. The door opened below and a man walked slowly up the stairs. When he reached the top, he paused.

"Hi. Is this where I'm supposed to sit?"

"Yes," Tobias replied, "if you don't mind." He heard the chair move slightly.

"No, not at all. Are you Tobias?"

"Yes, I am. What's the nature of your problem?"

"Actually, I don't have one. I know of the healer and want to speak with him, if you don't mind." The voice was confident and articulate. Tobias judged he was an educated man.

"About what?"

"About his healing ability. I'd like to speak with him about his gift."

"I'm sorry, I can't allow that. We get many requests like yours, but we prefer to use the healer's time more profitably. We have nothing to hide, it's just that we've been through this kind of thing many, many times over the years. He's been looked at by every medical and psychical research group you can think of, along with curiosity seekers galore. It's one of the main reasons I'm here."

"I admit to being curious as well, but I'm a medical doctor and—"

"Stop right there, doctor. Your group is one of the most feared and worst offenders. In his early years the healer was interviewed and examined by every type of doctor that was ever invented. He even welcomed them. They prodded and poked at him incessantly. One group even wanted to take biopsies! Can you imagine that! What the hell would that possibly accomplish? They treated him like a freak, and not one of them ever admitted to any definable results, other than to conclude that he might be genuine."

"I don't think you understand. I don't intend to—"

"I understand more than you realize, doctor. This man has cured cancer, blindness, bone deformities and a list of maladies that goes on and on, and not one of those goddamned doctors or researchers ever conceded that it was the work of the healer. They always looked to some other unknown cause. I was the one who finally called a halt to it all of that crap. No, there is no way I'm—"

"Tobias, please...I was cured by the healer." Tobias stopped abruptly.

"What? When?"

"A long time ago. I was a sixteen-year old kid with a congenital heart condition. Doctors gave me a year or two at most. I was told I could drop dead at any moment. My mother heard of the healer and brought me to him. I was not only cured, but I was profoundly affected. That was the reason I went into the medical field. The healer moved away shortly afterward. A lot of years have gone by, and I never knew of his whereabouts until recently, when one of my patients was cured by him. I wasn't sure it was him until I heard your name mentioned. Your name was the one that I remembered. As I recall, you were blind, and those dark glasses tell me you still are."

Tobias was taken aback, and didn't speak for several moments.

"I see. What's your name?"

"Poulette…Ray Poulette. Would you mind if I brought the chair closer?"

"No, whatever you wish," Tobias replied. The doctor took the chair and brought it near the desk and sat down.

"I don't remember you," Tobias commented, "but I'm sure it was a long time ago. Where did this take place?"

"Barrington, Illinois."

"Yes, we were there for awhile. We had to leave there and moved on to Massachusetts, then here. That was a long, long time ago. What kind of doctor are you?"

"A heart surgeon. What else?" Tobias smiled.

"Well, even so, doctor, what do you hope to accomplish?"

"To thank him, if nothing else. I'm a believer, Tobias, not a skeptic. I'm curious about the mechanics of what he does, which is the scientist in me. I can't help that, but I have no doubt he cured me by some miraculous means. Please, Tobias, I need to see him."

"I'd really rather not, doctor. He's not well, and his time is limited. I don't want it taken up with—"

"What's wrong with him?" Poulette asked, with genuine concern in his voice.

Tobias explained. "I see, I understand, but that's all the more reason I need to see him. I won't take more than a few minutes, Tobias. Please." Tobias moved his hands back and forth on the desktop and did not reply for a few seconds.

"Very well, doc, but you should know he doesn't want any medical treatment whatsoever, so please refrain from offering any assistance. As I explained to you, he knows he's dying, and he's ready to pass."

"You have my word, Tobias."

"Wait here, Doc." With that, Tobias stood and entered the back room. The healer opened his eyes and smiled.

"There's a man here to see you. He was one of your cures a number of years ago. He just wants to thank you and say hello. Is that alright?"

The healer patted Tobias' hand, a signal that it was permissible. It was a familiar request. Tobias got the doctor and brought him into the room and introduced him. The doctor shook the healer's hand and sat down.

"Well, I'll leave you two alone," Tobias said as he put his hand on the doctor's shoulder and squeezed slightly to get his attention. "Not too long, Doctor Poulette, as we agreed."

"No, I promise, and thanks." Tobias left the room.

Chapter Eight

About ten minutes passed, during which Tobias felt more and more anxious. As he was about to rise from his chair, the door finally opened and the doctor emerged. He wiped tears from his eyes and sat down.

"Thanks, Tobias. I told him who I was and why I was here. He was very pleased that I became a doctor, and told me it was his belief that all of the people he cured, no matter how slight their problem, had a purpose in life, and that each one was destined to be changed in some way by the cure. He has a very deep faith. I believe in God as well, but even I sometimes wonder if my cure was more natural than miraculous. If nothing else was accomplished, talking to him has renewed my faith in God, and my belief in what He accomplished with me. The healer is an extraordinary man…extraordinary."

"You have no idea, doctor…no idea. Lourdes can't hold a candle to him." Tobias then explained why it was necessary to move every few weeks.

"I see," the doctor replied. "I didn't attempt to examine him as I promised you, but my visual observation confirms what you told me. The man is dying. I had all I could do to restrain myself from offering help. As for moving him, Tobias, I wouldn't recommend you move him anywhere, unless he dramatically improves." Before Tobias could reply, the downstairs door opened.

"They're becoming more frequent already," Tobias commented to no one in particular. They both listened to a confusion of sounds emanating from below, and at first Tobias was unable to determine how many people had entered. It became clear as he heard a man grunting and a wheelchair thumping its way up the stairs. He perceived a second, then a third person ascending behind the wheelchair. "Three people walking, and a fourth in a wheelchair," he commented. "One of those on the stairs is a woman in high heels." The doctor rose and went to the head of the stairs. He shook his head in admiration as he confirmed what Tobias had determined.

"Do you need some help there?" the doctor asked.

"No, no," came the reply. "I can get her up there okay." The doctor returned to the desk.

"Mind if I stay for this one?"

"No, but just this one. Very often there is highly personal information given, and more than one person makes them uncomfortable."

The entourage finally managed to reach the head of the stairs. The doctor observed a thin, middle-aged woman in the wheel chair. A young man held the chair. Another man, also middle-aged, and a young woman accompanied them. The young man behind the wheelchair spoke first.

"We're looking for the healer. Are we in the right place?"

"Yes, this is the right place. My name is Tobias. Have a seat and please tell me why you're here."

"This is my mother, Renée," the young man said, gesturing to the woman in the wheelchair. "I'm her son, Philip."

"How do you do?" the woman said, cheerfully. "Are you the healer?"

"No, I guess I would be the dragon at the moat," Tobias answered, smiling. "I screen people who are seeking help." Everyone laughed.

"I see. Well, I would have called first, but we had no phone number. I just wanted to meet him today and see if he would accept me. I know there would be a cost, and other details to consider, but I did want to speak with him about my problem."

"Okay. I assume you're the one in the wheelchair."

"Yes…yes, of course," she answered, looking puzzled. The man behind the wheelchair spoke.

"I think Tobias is blind, Mom. Is that correct, Sir?"

"Yes, it is, and I'm assuming that does very little for your confidence in the healer. It's a long story, and not something I usually discuss. Who else is here? I heard high-heel shoes and another man coming up the stairs."

"This is my dad, Prentice, and my sister Arlene." All exchanged greetings with Tobias.

"And I'm doctor Poulette," the doctor offered. "I'm not here in any professional capacity. I was one of the healer's cures, and just came by to say hello. If you'd rather I leave to have some privacy, I'd be glad to go." All agreed it would not be necessary.

"Tell me, Renée," Tobias inquired, "how long have you been crippled?"

"A little over three years. I used to be a diving instructor, and I fractured my lower spine in a diving accident. I injured a nerve and lost the use of my legs."

More questions and answers were exchanged, followed by Tobias' explanation of the procedure. It was agreed that Renée and her husband would be the only ones allowed in the room with the healer. They went inside and closed the door.

During the next fifteen minutes, Tobias exchanged pleasantries with the son and daughter, fending off any references to his own disability. The doctor questioned the children further about their mother's injury, what doctors she had seen, what their prognosis had been. While he was intensely curious about the outcome of the healing, Tobias was fearful for the healer. Finally the doorknob turned, and everyone looked anxiously toward the door.

Renée was wheeled out by her husband. She was smiling broadly, but shook her head back and forth to indicate nothing had happened. Tobias listened to sounds of disappointment from the family.

"You may feel something later on, but I doubt it," Tobias said. "This happens sometimes, Renée, and I have no idea why."

"That's alright, Tobias," she answered. "I didn't have that much hope, so I'm not greatly disappointed. Perhaps I just didn't have enough faith."

"That has nothing to do with it," Tobias replied softly. "I've seen extreme skeptics get healed. I have no explanation for you, Renée. I'm sorry, I wish I did." Renée smiled generously and then signaled her husband to leave. Poulette stood to go.

"I was hoping I would see a cure. That one would have been dramatic."

"Sorry, Doc, that's the way it goes. Shake your faith in God, does it?"

"Yes, I must admit it does, but I still believe. I came out of the healer's room with my faith fully restored and after watching this, it's already shaken. Makes me wonder of God is putting me to the test. Mind if I see the healer again?"

"No, but I'll go with you." They entered the room, and Tobias went directly to the healer, sat down, and took his outstretched hand.

"There was no cure, was there?"

"No," Tobias replied, "I don't think so…I don't think so. How are you?"

"I'm fine. I didn't think anything happened. I didn't feel anything. I tried three times." Poulette went to the bed and knelt down on one knee. He took the hand that Tobias released.

"I'll just say goodbye again," he said, covering the healer's hand with his own. The healer smiled at him.

"You have an ulcer, don't you? It's probably work-related."

"Yes," Poulette chuckled, "I do, and you're probably right." The healer squeezed Poulette's hand. Poulette felt a reaction in his stomach.

"Not any longer. Thank you for stopping to see me. It means a great deal to me." Poulette stood, ashen-faced.

"A bit of grace and reaffirmation for you," Tobias said, smiling at him. The doctor nodded.

"Yes, it is…it certainly is." He then said his goodbyes and left. Tobias returned to his desk, crumbled another slice of bread, and put it on the outside window sill.

Chapter Nine

Another twenty minutes passed before the door opened again.

"Hello," a man shouted, "anyone up there?"

"Yes," Tobias shouted back. He heard a man take the stairs two at a time, and was annoyed when he continued across the room to the desk.

"Didn't you wonder why the chairs are at the head of the stairs, and not near my desk?" Tobias asked brusquely.

"But there is a chair beside your desk. What are you, blind? Would you rather I sat elsewhere?"

"I'm sorry," Tobias replied, "I forgot there was a chair here. How can I help you?" The man was young, his voice self-assertive. Tobias' first impression was not good. The man's brashness and overall demeanor bothered him.

"I'm guessing you're not the healer, are you?"

"No, I'm not. My name is Tobias. I work for the healer. How can I help you?"

"Mind taking those dark glasses off, Toby? I like to see a man's eyes."

"Yes, I do mind, and I prefer to be called Tobias. Once again, what's the nature of your problem?"

"Whew! Touchy! I don't have a problem, I have a solution."

"Are you selling something? What's your name, please?"

"I like to call myself Solarum. I took that name ever since I found out I had the gift."

"Solarum?"

"Yeah, you know, it's a Harry Potter spell, a blast of light. I think it's cool, and it fits what I can do." Tobias gave out with a loud sigh. The man continued. "I've heard about the healer, and I've come with a proposition. Now, don't say no till you hear me out." Tobias judged the man to be in his late twenties. He smelled of cheap cologne.

"What gift is that?" Tobias asked, reluctantly.

"I can heal. My gift is not so much physical healing as spiritual. I mean, man, it just radiates from my fingers. I always knew I had it, but I just kept denying it, ya know what I mean? When I touch someone's hands, I can actually feel their pain. I just know, somehow. And then I release energy through my fingers, and heal their pain."

"That's nice," Tobias replied, "but this healer cures physical ills and—"

"I asked you to hear me out. I can add a valuable service here. Think of it. One stop for physical and spiritual healing. I wouldn't ask for much of a cut, just enough to make a decent living."

"What is your given name?"

"I prefer Solarum. That is my name now."

"Well, Sol, the healer doesn't charge anything. If we could use you, I certainly wouldn't object to a fifty-fifty split of that. Now, please leave." Tobias winced as the door opened downstairs. He heard light, steady footsteps, but got no read on the gender. Solarum strode to the head of the stairs.

"Hi there, ma'am. Are you here to see the healer?"

"Yes, yes I am," the woman replied as she reached the head of the stairs.

"Well, come right over. I'd like to introduce you to Toby. Toby works for the healer. What's your name please?"

"Christine," the woman answered, looking puzzled as she allowed Solarum to lead her over to the desk. Tobias spoke in an authoritative voice.

"Leave, Solarum. Right now, or I call the police."

"Hey, hey, hey…at least let me show you what I can do for this woman. Here, ma'am, give me your hands."

"I said leave!" Tobias yelled. "Christine, this man does not work for the healer. Please pay him no mind." The woman looked anxiously back and forth between Solarum and Tobias. She pulled her hands away. "How can I help you?" Tobias asked.

"No, no…hold it!" Solarum shouted. "You're not even giving me a chance here. I can help this woman." Tobias reached for the phone and misjudged where it was. He fumbled a bit before he found it and lifted the receiver, then keyed in 911. The man quickly took the receiver out of Tobias' hand.

"Holy crap! You're blind, aren't you! You're a great advertisement for the healing guy. I wouldn't work here for anything. I've got my own reputation to consider. No need to call the cops, I'm leaving." Tobias heard the woman walking away as well.

"Christine…please wait. This man has nothing to do with the healer."

48

"I shouldn't have come up here. This is a sham. Godamnit, I should have listened to my sister...I should've listened. She said not to come here...she..." Tobias listened to her fading voice and the sound of her descending the stairs. Solarum stood at the head of the stairs and looked toward Tobias.

"That didn't go so well, did it?" he said, in a mocking voice. Tobias reached for the phone again. "Okay, okay, save it. I'm leaving this loony bin. Adios, Toby." Tobias felt relief as he listened to Solarum's quick receding steps. When the door opened below, he heard muffled voices as someone entered while Solarum was leaving. He recognized Stephanie's voice, and was relieved to hear her coming upstairs.

"Hi Toby, was that a cure that just walked out?"

"No, that was an idiot that just walked out. This is the second time I've felt threatened."

"Well, good news there," Stephanie replied, walking over to the desk. "The hardware store had nothing like you're looking for, but he knew another guy and so on. We have someone coming tomorrow to install a lock on the door, which is controlled by a coded key pad. The pad attaches to the door, so it's not electronic, but I'm sure you can master it. The best part is that it's all free." He heard Stephanie pulling items out of a paper bag, and smelled the aroma of hamburgers. He heard a glass jar sliding toward him. It nudged his arm. He found it with his hands and felt the shape. Stephanie giggled. "A little present for you, Toby." Tobias opened the jar and reached his hand inside. The odor of shelled peanuts reached him as he recognized their familiar shape. "Guess who they're for?" Stephanie asked. Tobias smiled broadly.

"My pigeons?"

Philip Birmingham

Chapter Ten

Stephanie left after reporting that the healer had eaten more than she expected. Almost a full hour passed before the door opened again. Tobias listened carefully. It was unquestionably a man, medium build. The steps were pronounced and suggested general good health. The man progressed steadily, reached the head of the stairs, and then stopped. He stood there, saying nothing for several seconds before walking toward Tobias. Tobias felt a twinge of concern.

"Yes, may I help you?" There was no reply. The stranger continued, then stopped abruptly in front of the desk. "Yes? Who are you? May I help you?" Still no reply. Tobias cocked his head slightly to one side, straining for any sounds. His body tensed. He felt air movement above him. "Sir, please tell me why you're..." It then occurred to Tobias what the problem was. The man was using sign language.

Tobias removed his glasses and stood, extending his open hands to the man. He felt the man's fingers touch his. He grasped them and put them against his eyes and slowly moved his head back and forth, to signify that he was blind. The man took Tobias' hands and held one of them against his cheek, nodding his head to indicate he understood. Then he placed Tobias' hands on his ears, lips, and finally his cheeks as he shook his head back and forth. Tobias put the man's hand to his cheek and nodded that he understood. The man was a deaf mute.

"Can you read my lips?" Tobias asked, reaching his hand forward. The man put it against his cheek and nodded. Tobias then sat down and explained the process, being careful to clearly form each word with his lips. The man again took Tobias' hand to his cheek and nodded. Tobias stood, asked the man to wait, then entered the healer's room.

"A man has come to be healed. He is a deaf mute. Are you able to see him?"

"Yes," the healer replied, with obvious effort in his voice.

"Very well," Tobias replied.

Tobias turned and gestured for the man to enter and sit in the chair beside the healer. Tobias left the room and went to his desk. A few minutes later the man emerged and walked halfway to the stairs, then collapsed to the floor, sobbing. The man had a voice, and it told Tobias that a cure had taken place. Tobias rose and walked carefully to him, following the sounds that the man was making. He knelt beside him.

"We're you cured?" The man grasped Tobias' hand firmly, and from force of habit pressed it against his cheek and nodded excitedly.

"I gan...I gan her...I gan her young, and I gan her myng owd voce...I gan her myng ownd voce...voce. I her youn...I her youn voce cleardly." Tobias stood and offered his hand to the man, who took it and stood. They returned to the desk and sat down. For the next fifteen minutes Tobias listened to the man's crying and efforts to form words, most of which he was able to divine.

He relayed to Tobias that his name was Jonas, that he was black, and worked as a janitor for a local bar, and that he had a wife and son. He repeatedly offered to donate money, which Tobias refused. When he asked permission to go back to the healer and thank him, Tobias reluctantly agreed. They entered the room, and Tobias stood there while the man strained to form words to express his gratitude. The healer held his hand and kept patting it reassuringly. Finally he left.

Tobias was exhausted. The day was slowly winding down, and he looked forward to Stephanie bringing supper and closing for the evening. He checked with the healer to see if he needed anything. He noted the healer's breathing was labored and spasmodic. The cure had taken its toll. He felt an ache in his throat. He gently patted the healer's arm and left the room, just in time to hear the door open downstairs.

Chapter Eleven

Tobias opened the window and spread peanuts on the sill as he listened to the familiar sounds of Stephanie climbing the stairs. The pigeons flew away, but two of them turned in mid-air when they reached the other side of the street and flew back, landing a couple of feet from Tobias. They were getting used to him. He smiled and closed the window.

"Hi, Toby."

"Hi, Steph. What's up, it's not supper time."

"I just wanted to tell you a man will be stopping by tomorrow afternoon to install a lock on the door, and show you how to use the keypad."

"Maybe we should hold off, Steph. That last cure took a lot out of him. He's bad Steph, and I don't think he's going to last much longer."

"I'm going to check on him. I'll be right back." Several minutes later she returned.

"You're right, Toby. I think I'll cancel it." Stephanie then sat down beside the desk. "The man is a saint, Toby, a living saint. I will never ever forget him for as long as I live."

"I don't think there will ever be one the likes of him again," Tobias added. The sound of the door downstairs caught their attention, prompting Stephanie to walk over to the head of the stairs. She observed a woman she estimated to be in her thirties, accompanied by a young girl, presumably the woman's daughter. The girl had an obvious spinal deformity, and was wearing an uncomfortable back brace. Her body was markedly twisted to one side, made worse by a contorted leg with its own heavy metal brace.

"Can you help us, please?" the woman asked. "Is the healer here? Is this the right place?" Stephanie looked dolefully toward Tobias, then answered the woman.

"Yes, yes," Stephanie said as she descended the stairs. Tobias could hear the dull clunking sounds of the leg brace as the young girl swung it onto each stair.

"Jesus Christ!" the woman exclaimed loudly, "Why the hell aren't you on the first floor! This is ridiculous! My God, why don't you people use your head?"

"I'm sorry," Stephanie replied, "I'm so, so sorry. These are donated premises, and we can't always get a first floor location."

"Bullshit! Bullshit! If I were in charge here you can bet your ass I would have a first floor location! There's no excuse for this…none whatsoever…no goddamned excuse!"

Tobias listened to an angry flow of constant complaints and expletives as the woman and Stephanie worked their way up the stairs. Between the two women talking back and forth, he heard anguished moans from the young girl. The sounds were familiar to him, confirming to Tobias that it was a spinal deformity. His emotions were conflicted. This could well be the one to end the healer's misery. Tobias suffered his own anguish listening to the progress on the stairs. His heart wanted to send them away, to spare the healer, but his intellect wanted the healer's pain over with, and an end to it all. The woman complained constantly in answer to Stephanie's efforts to apologize. The group finally reached the head of the stairs, where the young girl laid down on the floor on her side. The mother took a chair at the head of the stairs.

"And who are you? Are you the faith healer?" the woman asked, breathlessly.

"No, I'm not. My name is Tobias. I work for the healer."

"Do you have to have your offices on the second floor? This is inhumane! There's no excuse for this…no excuse whatsoever!"

"As Stephanie explained, these are donated premises, and we can't always get a first floor location. I'm sorry, you—"

"Skip the crap. What's the procedure here?" Tobias explained amidst fretful complaints and interruptions. During a third explanation, she cut him off abruptly. "Enough! What is the cost? I want to know how much before anything is attempted."

"There is no cost. Some people make a donation, but that's not required."

"Fine, fine...where's the healer? Is he in the other room in back of you? What do we have to do here?"

"Yes, but I need to speak with you first. May I ask your name?"

"Why, what do you need that for?"

"It's not absolutely necessary. You can remain anonymous. I really don't care. I do need the nature of your problem, however. I'm guessing this is a spinal deformity situation and …"

"Christ! What are you, blind? She has spinal bifida. She had an operation when she was born, and the spine has grown deformed. The back and leg braces should've been your first clue. They are there to try and straighten the bones as she grows and...why the hell am I telling you this? Use your eyes."

"I am blind, ma'am. I guessed it was a spinal deformity from the sounds you made coming up the stairs."

"Blind? Are you kidding me? For Christ's sake! I think I've made a mistake." Tobias first thought was to calm her fears, but he found himself wishing that she would leave. Stephanie spoke.

"Miss, I don't know how you heard about the healer, but he is genuine. Not everyone is healed, but he has a high percentage of cures. I'm assuming this is your daughter, and she's obviously severely disabled. What do you have to lose? It will cost you nothing." The woman sighed heavily.

"I'm sorry, it's just that it's been so frustrating. Yes, yes, she's my daughter, and I love her so much. She's in pain every day. She's still growing, and I have to tighten these braces periodically to force the bones back in position, and it's agony for both of us. Agony...agony every day. Once she even asked me to put her to death because of the pain." Stephanie stroked the woman's arm.

"What is your daughter's name? Would you tell us that?"

"Her name is Caroline. Mine is Mercedes. What's the procedure here? What do we do? Let's get to it."

Tobias again explained, stressing that if there was a cure, there would probably be more pain involved. He cautioned her about the healer's state of health. She gave out another exasperated sigh.

"This is shaping up real great. A blind assistant and a so-called healer who is in bad health. My God Almighty, what am I doing here?"

"As Stephanie just said, what have you got to lose?" Tobias replied. He found himself hoping desperately that she would leave, but reminded himself of his vow to the healer. He turned toward the sounds from the daughter. "Caroline, did you understand everything I said?"

"Yes...yes sir, I did. Will it hurt real bad?" The mother interrupted.

"Why is there pain if she's being healed? I don't get it. It doesn't make any sense to me."

"If there is a cure, it may very well hurt badly," Tobias answered. "That's why it's so important for you to understand." Caroline gave him an imploring look.

"Does he push down hard on my back, or my legs?"

"No, no he doesn't, Caroline. He just holds your hand, very softly. He may place his other hand on your back, or your legs, but it will also be very gently. I know all of this is hard to imagine, and hard to understand, but that's the way it works. Do you want to try?" Caroline looked up at her mother with questioning eyes.

"Yes," Mercedes replied, "we'll give it a try. What do we do again?" Tobias partially explained it all again, stressing the importance of not pulling away during the healing process because of the pain. Mercedes lifted her daughter and helped her toward the healer's room. Caroline moaned softly as she hobbled past Tobias. As they closed the door, Stephanie leaned over Tobias' desk and whispered, "I'm taking the coward's way out, Tobias. I'm leaving. I hope it works out for them." He heard the catch in Stephanie's voice.

"You're afraid for the healer, aren't you?"

"Yes, of course I am. I just don't want to be here. I sense this one's going to do it. Will you call me later at home?"

"I've been thinking the same thing, Steph. I'll call you either way." He felt Stephanie's hand stroke his own as she turned and left. As she descended, he heard her crying. He put his face in his hands and leaned on the desk.

Minutes passed in extreme slow-motion. Then he heard it, the familiar sounds he did not want to hear. He stood, but before he could move, the door opened forcefully behind him. As they exited the room, he heard Caroline falling to the floor.

"You bastards!" Mercedes yelled. "goddamn you all! goddamn you bastards! I never should have let myself be talked into this. The doctor was right, this is a sham! I hate you all! What the hell have you done to her?"

"Please," Tobias replied, "I told you that —"

"Shut the hell up, you goddamned fraud! I want my daughter out of here…now!" Caroline was moaning loudly as she attempted to get to her feet. "C'mon baby, you can do it…you can do it. I'm so sorry I did this, Caroline. Please forgive me…please! We'll get you to a hospital." Tobias interrupted.

"Mercedes, please listen to me. It's important. What's happening is—" .

"Shut up, you bastard! You bastard! What have you done to her? So help me God, I'm going to make you pay for this. You're going to pay dearly—all of you. I don't know what this scam is, but you haven't heard the last of it, I can guarantee you that! You bastards…you bastards." Tobias had had enough. He shouted at her.

"Unloosen the braces! That's the problem!" Mercedes looked suspiciously at Tobias.

"What the hell do you mean? What's—"

"Just shut your mouth and loosen the braces! That's the problem. Her spine is reforming, and the braces are preventing it. Loosen the braces, you idiot! Didn't you listen to what I told you, three different times?" There was a stunned silence, followed by the sounds of Mercedes quickly unhooking the brace on her daughter's back. Caroline groaned with relief, then rolled over and began crying.

Mercedes knelt beside her, crying profusely, and stroked her daughter's face.

"Oh, God…Oh, God, Caroline. Your back is straightening. I can see it…I can see it…Oh, God…Oh, God."

For the next several minutes, Tobias listened to the crying of the mother and daughter, intermingled with grateful remarks from Mercedes, but it fell on deaf ears. All he could think about was the healer's condition. He finally wished them well and heard them leave. As soon as they were gone, he went into the healer's room and sat down beside him, touching his hand. The healer lightly grasped his. The healer's breathing was spasmodic.

"How are you feeling? That was bad, wasn't it?" No reply. Tobias began to fear the worst. Then he heard a hoarse whisper.

"Yes…bad."

"Now can we stop? Now can we refuse any more? Enough is enough."

"No, Tobias, do not refuse. Say no more. You promised…you promised." Tobias gently squeezed his hand and released it.

"Very well, I promised…I'll keep my promise…I'll keep my goddamned promise. Goodbye, my friend…my brother." Tobias bit his lower lip to regain control. "This world did not deserve you." He wanted to say more, but his throat was constricted. The only reply was a gentle squeeze from the healer's hand. Tobias left the room. His throat muscles ached as he held back tears. His mind seemed to be elsewhere, deliberately removed, grasping the reality that the end was near. Then, several minutes later, it felt as if his heart stopped. It was a heavy, dismal, and most dreaded sound. The opening of the downstairs door.

Chapter Twelve

Tobias put his face in his hands and leaned on the desk on his elbows. He heard a man's footsteps. He then put his hands tightly over his own ears, to dull any further perceptions, to block out any hints of what might lie ahead.

"Tobias?" Tobias put his hands on the desk.

"Yes, yes…I'm Tobias."

"I would like to see the healer. The reason is…"

"No, I don't want to hear it. I don't want to know what your problem is, or anything about you." Tobias then quickly told the stranger what to expect, warning him about the healer's condition. The stranger did not reply, but rose and walked across the room, opened the healer's door, and entered.

Tobias leaned back in his chair. The cooing and shuffling of the pigeons reached his ears. He needed to do something routine. He picked up the jar of peanuts and opened the window. The pigeons did not scatter. He spread a generous amount on the sill and closed the window. Tears streamed down his cheeks. He felt other-worldly, as if his spirit was some other place in the universe.

The door opened and he heard the sounds of the man walking out of the healer's room, heading for the stairs. *Bastard!* Tobias thought. *A thank-you would have been in order, maybe even a small goddamned donation. Bastard! If you had any compassion at all, you would have refused to see the healer. Bastard!* Tobias returned to the desk and sat down. He decided that as soon as he heard the downstairs door close, he would check on the healer. He was anxious beyond description and knew, somehow, that the healer was gone. It was over.

He listened to the man's receding footsteps on the stairs. Something wasn't right. Some urgent thoughts were niggling at his mind, trying to intrude on his grief. A second later it occurred to him in a lightning burst of thought. It was the man's weight as he crossed the floor to enter the healer's room. When the man left the room, he was substantially heavier! It didn't match. Tobias didn't want to believe the conclusion, but he had no choice. A morbid fear sent sheer electricity through his body.

Tobias jumped to his feet, tripped over the chair beside the desk, and fell spread-eagle on the floor. He scrambled to his feet, feeling sharp pains in his right ankle. He limped and groped the air in all directions as he hobbled to the head of the stairs. The stranger had just reached the bottom.

"Stop! Stop! What are you doing? You can't do that! It will do you no good. Bring him back here! What the hell is the matter with you? He's dying…he's a dying man. He needs medical attention! Kidnapping him will do you no good, no good whatsoever. Bring him back, or I'm calling the police. Who in God's name do you think you are, and where the hell do you think you're taking him?"

Tobias' voice was at a fever pitch. The sound of his heart pounding in his ears hurt physically. The several seconds of silence that followed made him want to scream. He thought about going down the stairs and fighting the man, but how could he do it without injuring the healer? If the man left, Tobias decided he would go downstairs and go out on the sidewalk and yell for help. Finally, a reply came, in calm and measured tones.

"He's passed from this world, Tobias. I'm taking him home."

"Oh Christ…oh Christ! He has no home! Sonofabitch! Do you understand? He has no goddamned home! Dead? Jesus Christ…you sonofabitch! God damn you! Bullshit! He has no home. All of his relatives are long dead! Bring him back here, I'm begging you. We expected this, and we're prepared for it. Let me take care of him."

"I'm taking him home with me, Tobias."

"Like hell you are! Who are you? What's your name?" The reply was once again calm, the tone plaintive.

"Tobias, Tobias…you know who I am."

Tobias was struck dumb, unable to speak. More seconds passed. He opened his mouth again, but closed it. He did not hear the downstairs door open or close, but he knew they were gone. His legs trembled badly, and he collapsed on the stair. His left hand groped for the hand rail. This was simply too much for him to contemplate. He didn't know what to do. Then it happened.

There was a flickering of light. Specks flashed in his mind. He had encountered these many times before, the neural phenomena inside the mind of the blind, the false impression of light perception. But somehow these were different. They were growing rapidly, and expanding in his mind. Then impressions of dark swirling shapes, then more light, followed by discernable objects. He was beginning to see. The stairs and the walls came into view. He scanned back and forth, up and down, drinking it in. His vision was fully restored. He removed his left hand from the rail and examined it. He opened his eyes wide, blinked rapidly and marveled at the sight of his own hand as he flexed his fingers. He removed his dark glasses.

He tried to stand, but his legs felt like gelatin, and he fell back on the stairs. He tried again and pulled himself up on the handrail, then stood on shaking legs getting his bearings. He walked slowly back to his desk, taking in the room and his surroundings as he carefully picked up the overturned chair. He drank in every sight, every detail, every speck of airborne dust. He felt thrilling physical rushes up and down in his body. He reached the desk and had to sit down. There was a sharp pain in his right pinky finger. He looked down at it and watched it straighten before his eyes.

Sounds from the pigeons caught his attention, and he swiveled in his chair to look at them. There were three this time. Two were various shades of slate gray with white and lighter gray bars on their wings. One of them had accents of black, and the other an iridescent purple patch on its breast. The third was various shades of light and dark brown, with cream-white markings on its breast, wings, and tail feathers. He thought them all to be quite beautiful, and gave a slight smile. It wouldn't take long to tame them to his hand.

A noise downstairs brought his attention away from the window. He heard the door close and the sound of panting. He rose and walked to the head of the stairs. There was an overweight, elderly man in a rumpled suit standing in the hall, with his right hand on the rail. He wore a cannula on his face, which supplied oxygen to his nostrils by way of plastic tubes, and carried a portable oxygen tank over one shoulder. He looked up at Tobias. His face was ash-white.

"Do you need help getting upstairs?" Tobias asked.

The man shook his head that he did not, and then waved Tobias away. *A typical male*, Tobias thought as he returned to the desk. For the next several minutes he sat in stupor, unable to comprehend what had happened to him, and listened to the labored sounds of the old man ascending the stairs. The man would stop after two steps, sit on the stair tread, and gasp for air. Tobias glanced at his now normal right pinky finger, then over again at the pigeons.

Why? What did it all mean? Why did he get his sight back now? Tobias slowly scanned the room, back and forth, still relishing every visual perception. There were thrilling changes in his body that he did not understand. He felt like he was being created anew. Finally the man emerged at the head of the stairs, then slowly shuffled his way across the room and sat down heavily at the desk, waving a nicotine stained hand at Tobias to signify he needed time. Tobias waited. The man leaned forward, taking deep breaths and pursing his lips as he exhaled. It took several minutes, but some color finally began to appear in his face as he leaned back and took another deep breath.

"Are you the healer?" Tobias smiled, and in that moment he felt a final rush in his body, a flash of insight, an epiphany, and it was in that miraculous moment that he finally understood.

"Yes, I am…my name is Tobias."

THE END

ABOUT THE AUTHOR

Philip Birmingham's other works include "Poppy", about a hedgerow gnome who appears in the garden outside the dining room window one morning, is adopted by the family, then sets out to meet the rest of his new relatives. The book was written as a series of letters from Poppy to Mrs. B., and was to be mailed in several installments for the amusement of Philip's wife, Jean, (a/k/a Mrs. B.). Her world had been reduced to the garden outside the window after a debilitating illness, and she passed away before Poppy could make his first appearance. A year later, Philip completed the work as a tribute to her. "Poppy" returned from his travels and now resides on the hearth in the living room.

Philip Birmingham is the author of many short stories, poems, and anecdotes, and has several other books in the works. He resides in Queensbury, New York, with his favorite companions, two Maltese dogs named Lilliput and Gulliver. He can be reached through email at pbirmingham@roadrunner.com.

Poppy

Lilliput and Gulliver

www.ingramcontent.com/pod-product-compliance
Lightning Source LLC
Chambersburg PA
CBHW020022050426
42450CB00005B/596